Thank you Dad, for teaching me how to listen.

Thank you children, for reminding me to stop and listen.

Thank you Lily, for listening.

Shhhhhhh, baby. Listen.
Do you hear that?
It's a woodpecker swooping by.

Shhhhhhh, baby. Listen.
Do you hear that?
It's a box turtle rustling through the palmettos.

Shhhhhhh, baby. Listen.
Do you hear that?
Its an airplane flying by.

Shhhhhhh, baby. Listen.
Do you hear that?
It's the cicadas synchronizing in the branches.

Shhhhhh, baby. Listen.
Do you hear that?
It's a hog munching on acorns.

Shhhhhhh,
baby.
Listen.
Do you
hear that?
It's a swarm of mosquitoes buzzing.

Shhhhhhh, baby. Listen.
Do you hear that?
It's the frogs peeping from
the flag weeds.

Shhhhhh, baby. Listen.
Do you hear that?
It's the alligators bellowing
back and forth.

Shhhhhh, baby. Listen.
Do you hear that?
It's an airboat roaring
through the marsh.

Shhhhhh, baby. Listen.
Do you hear that?
It's the whippoorwill
calling out in the dark.

Shhhhhhh. Do you hear that?
Zzzzzzzzzzzz weeeeeeweeeeeweeeeweeee.
It's you little one, catching some zzzzzzzz's.

Sweet dreams, baby.

www.ingramcontent.com/pod-product-compliance
Lightning Source LLC
Chambersburg PA
CBHW040006040426
42337CB00033B/5236